**Dust and Prayers**

To Craig E. Mattson
with best wishes —

Faithfully yours,

Charles L. Bartow

Ps 150:6

# art for faith's sake series

SERIES EDITORS:

Clayton J. Schmit
J. Frederick Davison

This series of publications is designed to promote the creation of resources for the church at worship. It promotes the creation of two types of material, what we are calling primary and secondary liturgical art.

Like primary liturgical theology, classically understood as the actual prayer and practice of people at worship, primary liturgical art is that which is produced to give voice to God's people in public prayer or private devotion and art that is created as the expression of prayerful people. Secondary art, like secondary theology, is written reflection on material that is created for the sake of the prayer, praise, and meditation of God's people.

The series presents both worship art and theological and pedagogical reflection on the arts of worship. The series title, Art for Faith's Sake,* indicates that while some art may be created for its own sake, a higher purpose exists for arts that are created for use in prayer and praise.

OTHER VOLUMES IN THIS SERIES:

*Senses of the Soul* by William A. Dyrness

---

* "Art for Faith's Sake" is a phrase coined by art collector and church musician Jerry Evenrud, to whom we are indebted.

# Dust and Prayers

*Poems*

Charles L. Bartow

CASCADE *Books* · Eugene, Oregon

DUST AND PRAYERS
Poems

Art for Faith's Sake 2

Cascade Books
A Division of Wipf and Stock Publishers
199 W. 8th Ave., Suite 3
Eugene, OR 97401

www.wipfandstock.com

ISBN 13: 978-1-60608-110-5

*Cataloging-in-Publication data:*

Bartow, Charles L.

Dust and prayers : poems / Charles L. Bartow.

xvi + 70 p. ; 23 cm.

Art for Faith's Sake 2

ISBN 13: 978-1-60608-110-5

1. Poetry. 2. Christian Poetry, American. I. Title. II. Series.

PS3553.A2 B3 2009

Manufactured in the U.S.A.

*For my secretary, Lois F. Haydu,*

*Who walks in her integrity and*
*prays without ceasing.*

# Contents

# Acknowledgments

It is hard to know where to start. It is even harder to know where to stop. There are so many to thank! There is, in fact, everyone to thank, for everyone I've ever known in person or in print has written something into me that has found its way out into what I myself have written. Nevertheless, a few must be mentioned as representing the rest.

The trustees of Princeton Theological Seminary, president Iain R. Torrance and dean Darrell L. Guder administer a generous sabbatical leave policy. Thus I have been allowed the space and time to think and write. My seminary colleagues in Preaching, Speech Communication in Ministry, and Worship made sure all the academic bases were covered while I was away. Thanks then to Michael A. Brothers, Sally A. Brown, Nancy Lammers Gross, James F. Kay, Henry Robert Lanchester, Cleophus J. LaRue, Jr., J. Randall Nichols, and Luke A. Powery.

My mentor, colleague, and treasured friend, William Brower, is owed a great debt of gratitude for decades of patient instruction and a lively exchange of views. Michael G. Hegeman, a brilliant composer, accomplished biblical scholar, and practical theologian, has set to music some of my poetic efforts. Martin Tel, C. F. Seabrook Director of Music at Princeton Seminary, graciously has conducted performances of carols and anthems I composed. His predecessor, the late David Weadon, did the same. The musical artistry of these men has encouraged me to believe that there is, or ought to be, implicit melody—and even choreography—in every poem.

Especial thanks are due to Clayton J. Schmit, Arthur DeKruyter/ Christ Church Oak Brook Associate Professor of Preaching, and academic director of the Brehm Center for Worship, Theology, and the Arts at Fuller Theological Seminary. Without his unflinching support and wise counsel, this exploration in poetry for faith's sake could not have been managed at all. So too deep thanks are owed to Cascade Books for their superb professional contribution to the publication of this little book.

My wife, Ruth Paula Goetschius Bartow, ever and always at my side in prayer and in wise, affectionate conversation, takes my thought and my life, even at their worst, and makes the most of them, her every breath to the praise of God's glory. My daughter, Rebecca J. Bartow, read every poem in this volume with great care and suggested needed corrections of both form and content. She is a better critic than she is willing to admit. Not least, Lois F. Haydu, for seventeen years my secretary, cannot be thanked sufficiently for all she does to enable my studies, my writing, my teaching, and my pastoral service to the church. Appropriately *Dust and Prayers* is dedicated to her.

## Taking the Risk: Poetry for Faith's Sake

Why not poetry for faith's sake? Long ago an objection might have been raised, but no longer. No longer do aesthetic theorists speak of art for art's sake, music for music's sake, painting for painting's sake, poetry for poetry's sake. Nothing is for its own sake, not even love, not even love of God.

Of course one had better not love God for the benefits such love entails, any more than one dare cherish a friendship for its benefits, or a spouse or a child for their endearing qualities, the happiness they bring. Our loved ones expect to be loved not for gain, but for all they mean to us beyond and without calculation.

Nevertheless God is love, and loving God has its benefits, all the more to be cherished because they are freely given. It has been said that the Holy Trinity's love of its very nature overflows. You can no more love God for nothing then than you can breathe without receiving the benefits of respiration. So it is in a more modest way with a friend's love, with spousal love, with the love of a child. No love is to no purpose. No artistic enterprise—however accomplished or clumsy—serves only itself, turns only to itself in self-congratulation.

If a poem is read, or better spoken, and—dare I say it?—is in some sense enjoyed, should the poet complain that his or her work has been abused? If a poem speaks of fading love, shall the poet be crestfallen if that fading affection—somehow, all unintended—reminds someone of a love that does not fade, that is enduringly faithful, beautiful, and holy? If a poet's praise of nature stirs up somewhere the praise of nature's God, shall the poet cry, "Foul! That is not what I meant! It is not what I *could* have meant!" The poet may thus complain, but the complaint will be to no avail, for when the ink of the poet is turned to blood in the reader's or speaker's act of reading and speaking, there is no telling what intentions beyond those of the poet may be realized. Not less than what was meant, but other and more than what was meant may be added to what was meant. Faith may make of unfaith nourishment for its own soul. So poetry may be for faith's sake no matter the poet's own faith or lack of it. Archibald MacLeish famously observed, "A poem should not mean / But be." Should he object that someone found his remark meaningful?

George Steiner in *Real Presences* has noted at length, and with a daunting display of erudition, that all works of art imply Presence.[1] The thought is not out of harmony with the Reformed doctrine of extraordinary means of grace. The ordinary means of grace—to which human beings are bound, though God is not so bound—are word, sacrament, and prayer. But, as theologian Karl Barth has noted, God may speak through a dead dog, or, we might add, a dead letter, or a dead poet, or a poet's long dead and buried worst poems, not to mention the poet's still living and breathing better poems.

Yet more there is the Christian doctrine of the "contrary sign": Holy Presence attested in what seems to suggest God's real absence. However one understands the presence of Christ in the Lord's Supper, for instance, whether through transubstantiation or as spiritual presence in the believing community, the presence of Christ is vouchsafed to the faithful with bread and wine, so congregants come to believe, and, in believing, to know.

Of course it could be argued, *has* been argued, that such belief is blind and such knowledge no knowledge at all. Yet, on the other hand, it could be argued, *has* been argued, that *un*belief is blind and so fails to come to know what it might. Now plainly a poem is not a sacrament, but, following the logic of sacramental thought, can one at will banish from the word of the poet the Presence of the Word, or, from the poet's work, even if composed in unbelief, what faith may make of it? If W. H. Auden was right in claiming that "poetry makes nothing happen," that seems unlikely.

We speak of atheism, of disbelief, of unfaith. Some, in fact, have alleged of late that God is not great. But atheism defines itself, must define itself, by theism, and so it knows what theism is. It rejects theism, but knows full well what it rejects. So does disbelief assume—and know—belief. The refusal of belief, as a result, by necessity entails the possibility of coming to belief. Unfaith likewise implies faith, defines itself by what it denies. If the faithful therefore at times fear the possibility of a loss of

---

1. George Steiner, *Real Presences* (Chicago: University of Chicago Press, 1991).

faith, the unfaithful likewise from time to time fear coming into possession of—fear becoming possessed by—faith.

Too, saying that God is not great entails the belief, the faith, the knowledge that greatness has its home somewhere, has a source, so to speak in Greatness, a God-term if there ever was one. Negations always suggest the presence, the greatness of what is negated. And words put to ill use entail awareness of the better use to which they might have been put.

Pilate's sneering inscription above the head of the crucified Christ makes the point: "Jesus of Nazareth, the King of the Jews" (John 19:19). He was importuned to change the inscription. But he insisted, "What I have written, I have written" (John 19:22). The whole act has a mocking, poetic quality to it, imperial pronouncement to cow the will of any who might call it into question. Nevertheless the ages have read in the epithet the truth to which Pilate, while denying it, was accountable. A *poesis* wrought in disbelief, even in contempt of faith, found itself in service to what it held in contempt. That is the irony and grammar of the gospel at every turning.

The poems in this little book are intended for faith's sake. But the poet's intentions may "come a cropper" given the possibility of readers' contrary intentions, though he hopes, he prays that that may not be so. Yet who can say? Who can tell? Poetry for the sake of anything takes its risks. Poetry for faith's sake therefore also is put at risk.

## Strange Dust

*Let me take it upon myself to speak to the Lord, I who am*
*but dust and ashes.*
—GENESIS 18:27

*It is strange dust that considers itself to be dust.*
—GEORGE ARTHUR BUTTRICK

A text of poetry may seem a peculiar thing for a preacher to attempt. A sermon, after all, is straight talk, but a poem, as Emily Dickinson famously remarked, often aims "to tell it slant." Too, proclamation of the gospel is, or ought to be, "through faith for faith" (Romans 1:17), while a poem may sound an agnostic note. Moreover a preacher may or may not be steeped in literature. A poet, on the other hand, is expected to be— some might say is required to be—among the first rank of the literati.

Yet the preacher and the poet clearly have one thing in common. They deal in words, verbal gestures that imply vocal and physical gesture. The text of the sermon implies the event of proclamation, the text of the poem implies what Susanne Langer called its "virtual life." And if Emerson was anywhere near the mark when he insisted "every word was once a poem," the preacher must be a poet in the making of the sermon, and the poet the preacher's tutor in crafting words for the Word.

More so the poet than the rhetor, for the rhetor aims to make something happen, to get a message across. The rhetor intends to teach, to delight, to persuade. But the poet, like the preacher, attests a happening. A bolder equation: perhaps the text of a poem, like the text of a sermon, is nothing more nor less than the dust of a prayer stirred to life, as Auden put it, "in the valley of its saying," a moment's praise or lament, brief as a cloud, about the lips of an alien hospitality, not petition, not intercession, not a plea for results, only a statement of what is or could be—absent the imperative, the real presence of a fragile indicative. This preacher, then, prayerfully has attempted the text of poetry that follows. What if anything gets stirred to life out of the dust of his prayer remains to be seen and heard.

Charles L. Bartow
Princeton, NJ
May 23, 2007

## ALONE I HEAR YOU SPEAK

*(For Paula)*

The wood is solitude of sound and sight,
And here the ear can listen, just as light
Can cut a shaft through limbs and leaves to grass,
To tinge bright gold the quiet green I pass.
Alone, I hear you speak in every blade;
Your voice the glistening hush upon the glade.

## ATONEMENT

This August's crepe myrtle are brilliant pink,
Having been fed in the fall and the spring,
Having been pruned and mulched through the winter,
Having been blanketed too in piled leaves
Wire-fenced around, packed, to hold in the warmth.
Love and hope conspired to effect the deed,
Her love of beauty and her hope in life,
Her precise caring. She knew heedless hands
Years before had planted these blossomed shrubs
Too far north. No harm had been intended,
But sweet sincerity and sentiment
Had done their eager work without much thought;
So her labor was required to set right
What artless good intentions got all wrong.

# I DREAMED A FOSTER CHILD

Footprints in the snow lighter than a breath,
Breath candy sweet upon the cheek of age,
Age-kissed innocence in the eye of youth,
Youth's shadow bright across the face of time.

Time, brim full of promises made and kept,
Kept infant hope alive and fostered dreams,
Dreams, foster-parented, to chase The Dream,
The Dream he had who said, "I have a dream."

I have a dream that one day . . . who can tell?
Who can tell what comes of dreams not deferred,
Deferred and left to fester in the sun,
The sun-filled dreams in rainbow tears of joy?

"Before I formed you in the womb," God said,
"I knew you." Rainbow-promised child of God.


Note: *I Dreamed A Foster Child* was commissioned (without fee) by Emma R. Marshall for celebration of the Fairfax County, VA, Foster Care and Adoption Program.

## OREMUS

Just as you taught us
    To love you Lord,
        So, at length,
We would pray to you
    With heart and soul
        And mind and strength.

# QUESTIONS OF THE SOUL

Will I ever love the Lord
With all my heart, soul, mind, and strength;
Will I ever seek the truth
And thereby come to know at length
Love that, loved not, loves the more
My loveless heart, soul, mind, and strength,
Truth that, sought not, still is true
And to be known as true at length?

Will I ever hate my life
Fashioned with heart, soul, mind and strength;
Will I ever dare to die
To self and thereby gain at length
Life, that fashioned not by me
With all my heart, soul, mind, and strength,
Lies hidden with Christ in God
To be revealed with him at length?

## THE WORLD'S PASSING

It seems as though the world's passing me by,
And what is more I'm not so sure I care.
The setting up of virtual domains,
The hateful, braying blogger sites and all,
They try the patience of the saint I'm not.
I sigh for patient thoughts, hand-written notes,
Articulations of the risk, the dare
Of personal truth signed off on, the cry
Of heart to heart against the evil day
When hearts no longer matter, will is all:
The will to win or ruin, rule or kill.
I've seen it in the smallest child's play,
And in adult play-stations that appall.
The passing world's all gain, or loss of heart.

## BRAIN POWER

Our mind entire is in our brain we're told,
To instance all we think and feel and do,
Our thoughts of God, our deepest hatreds too,
Our self-regard, our altruisms bold
Or timid, friendships forged, or friendships sold
To purchase place in dreams we'd have come true
When, tired of where we've been, we seek some new
Adventure with companions who have hold
Of what we'd now attain. Still, this we own:
That all we think and feel and do we set
Our minds to. Instance: "Use your brains!" we say,
As though our minds, our brains had not alone
Determined what their use might be. We vet
Somehow our thoughts, and make their must our may.

## TACIT PARADOX

It's said that we know more than we can say,
Yet say more than we know each passing day.

## BASSAMAT AL-FARAH
*(The Smile of Joy)*

A sonnet composed following the terrorist destruction of the World Trade
Center Towers in New York City, and related atrocities of September 11, 2001.
The smile of joy on the lips of suicide bombers indicates their belief that their
death is a martyr's death. Such a death is their guarantee of entrance into
paradise.

Last night my mother came to me in dreams
To tuck me in and help me say my prayers,
As long ago she used to climb the stairs
To where I'd lie awake, in dread of schemes
Drawn up by attic demons who, with screams
Of terror, hauled young children to their lairs
And turned them into demons with no cares—
No souls for caring. Mother's prayers cast beams
Of searing light against the nightmare dark,
And still they do, as I attempt to pray
My rage at careless demons in the sky,
*Bassamat al-farah* etched cold and stark
Upon their lips, who crash in flame and flay
Grown children's souls for whom fierce mothers cry.

## SEASONS OF LOVE

This blue pansy, velvet soft
Yet hardiest of flowers,
Gaily shines through winter ice,
Thaws my heart and wins my smile.

And you, my dearest, softer yet,
Though fierce heat and cold oppose,
Win from me this solemn vow:
To cherish you through every clime.

## REAL PRESENCE

Hear in the late spring breeze
That barely stirs the trees
The sighing of a heart
That gives my soul a start!
My love is surely there,
Warmth of the late spring air,
She, for whose touch I long,
Kissing my lips with song!

## LOVE'S DUTY

Some say they have no duty but to love,
Some that they've no love except their duty.
I say a love that's duty is not love,
And yet more loveless love not duty-bound.

# ON TAHOE'S STEEP

*(The Sierra Nevada Peaks Above South Lake Tahoe to the East)*

On Tahoe's steep and storm-washed eastern slope
The hemlock, pine, and fir have come to cope,
Even to thrive, with soilless rock for food.
Through centuries of waste these trees have stood
Rock-rooted, sure, drawing sustenance there
Where all that can be seen seems lifeless, bare,
While far below these steepled fastnesses
Lives, weathered less hard, find in trespasses
Of the frontier of the wild and the tame
Their own forms of sustenance: fish and game,
Free play upon the lake. Farther below,
The Sacramento valley, where we grow
Our rice, our soy, our sugar beets, our corn,
All in a fertile soil never outworn,
Washed down from heights long dead, but for the stir
Of wind through rock-fed hemlock, pine, and fir.

# FRIENDSHIP, SQUIRRELS, AND WIVES

"Rats with fuzzy tails," my friend, Ted, calls them,
Joking, yet with factual precision.
"Rodents, that is what they are, and pesky.
Were it legal I'd dispatch them quicker
Than a tail-flick." "But," I say, "my wife thinks
They're so cute, poised, sitting, eating, happy
As the day is long. And you'd dispatch them,
Leaving me to deal with her sorrow,
Her dismay!" Here Ted breaks out that famous
Grin he learned in the Marines. "A friendship
Only goes so far," he chortles. "Squirrels
Mark the end of it for sure." I chortle
Back at him: "Why Ted," I say, "Did not I
See your Freda just this morning feeding
Squirrels on the quad, beside the oak tree?
Called one Wilbert, I believe. A good name,
Cute name, right name for a squirrel. Paula
Would have called him that had she been feeding
Squirrels cashews. 'Wilbert food for certain'
She'd have said." Still smiling, Ted draws up his
Fist from off his hip and fast and dead on
Aims his index finger at my smiling
Heart. "You got me there," he says; and cries out
"Bang! I told you squirrels ended friendship."
I poured Ted and me another scotch. "To
Friendship, and to shooting squirrels. Cute rats
They may be, and fuzzy-tailed, but not worth
Friendship, or those cashews, or a scotch. Drink
Up," I say, "drink up." "But," Ted replies, "Shh,
Shh! I think I hear our wives. They're coming."

# LITTLE HAROLD

A Meditation on the *Imago Dei*

*So God created humankind in his image,*
    *in the image of God he created*
        *them;*
    *male and female he created*
        *them   (Genesis 1:27, NRSV).*


My cousin, Little Harold,
Sat near the kitchen door,
Twisting in his fingers
The string he always held.
Harold's older sister, Jean,
Asked him, "What is that?"
"String, string," Harold replied,
Trying hard, it seemed,
To get it right.
Jean smiled assurance,
But Little Harold sat
As he always sat,
Face blank, eyes dim,
Head tipped left a bit,
Shoulders slumped, legs still;
Twentyish year old man,
Mind of a little child.

I sat anxious in place
At the kitchen table,
A child about nine.
Jean pointed at me
And asked Harold,
"Who is that?"

*(continued on p. 16)*

"Chumsy, Chumsy," Harold said.
Once again Jean smiled,
Smiled assurance.
I grew less anxious;
But Little Harold sat
As he always sat,
Face blank, eyes dim,
Head tipped left a bit,
Shoulders slumped, legs still,
Fingers twisting, twisting
The string he always held.

My dad came in, and called,
"Lets go to Hadley Field."
Old time air shows there
Thrilled us children,
Pleased our parents too.
So off we went,
Little Harold and I,
My cousin, Jean,
And my dad.
We stood at the runway fence.
A biplane took off.
Little Harold cried,
"Plane!  Plane!"
His eyes wide, bright.
He smiled, let go his string,
Pointed, and said again,
"Plane!  Plane!"
Jean smiled, I smiled;
My dad smiled too.

*(continued on p. 17)*

16

Later—who knows why,
Was it the string he'd let go?—
Little Harold
Threw a tantrum,
Fingers clenched,
Arms, muscled as a grownups,
Flailing, and his face
Wild with tears and rage.
My dad looked anxious;
I stood frozen, speechless.
Jean clasped Little Harold
From behind, tight,
And brought him down hard.
Harold's fists pummeled the air.
Jean, almost in a whisper,
Ordered, "Harold! Harold!
Stop! Calm down!"
Little Harold stopped.
Had he stopped for love,
For the sense he'd not prevail?
Who could say?
Not Harold for sure,
Not Jean, not my dad.
I was too young to know.
Sixty years since,
I still don't know,
Can't even guess.

*(continued on p. 18)*

Decades passed
Without my seeing Harold.
I grew up, grew old.
I learned, at last,
Harold had been placed
In a state home.
There, among his peers,
Sedated now and then,
He spent uneventful days
Tantrum free.
Toward the end, I'm told,
He lay curled up
Like a fetus
Still-born, string in hand,
Eyes dim, head tipped left a bit,
Shoulders slumped, legs still,
Fortyish year old man;
Mind of a child—gone.

AUTHOR'S NOTE: Little Harold and his sister, Jean, were in fact my cousins, and events such as those mentioned in this poem actually happened. With the exception of Harold and Jean, though, characters, and venues of action too, have been conflated, and time compressed to move along the narrative, and to intensify the drama of the *imago Dei* biblically attested in Genesis 1:27, and, in our always poignant relationships, lived out.

## REGARDING THE GIFT WITHOUT THE GIVER

*(Practical Wisdom as Enlightened Self-interest)*

"The gift without the giver is bare,"
But if the giverless gift is there
For the taking, I'll take it happily,
And be glad the giverless gift is free.

NOTE: The phrase, "the gift without the giver is bare," is from: James Russell Lowell, *The Vision of Sir Launfal*, Part Second, viii.

## POSTMODERN CONCEPTION

Human life begins not at conception,
Much less at birth, but in the mind of God.
To this thought most moderns take exception,
But modern thought is not our avant-garde.
Twelfth-century pride birthed its affection,
Framed its mind. *Post*-moderns give God the nod.

## ALEXANDER'S CAROL

*(In Honor of Alexander James Royster Marshall,*
*Born January 29, 1987)*

Sing to our Sovereign Savior, Christ Jesus,
Born in a stable, lowly.
Shepherds adore him, wise men come laud him,
Mary's son, God's Child, holy.

This is the day we've waited and longed for,
Day of salvation glorious.
So we rejoice to lift up our voice and
Join in the mighty chorus.

Light years from now the cosmos resounds with
Glad anthems never ending.
Stable-born babe, almighty to save, this
Is your deserved thanksgiving.

REFRAIN
*(Sung after each stanza)*

Shout for joy all you heavenly choirs!
People of earth, your praises
Offer now, for this blessed babe,
Full of God's love and grace, is
Bringing to old and young, women, men,
The power to be God's children,
Reigning in life and death, free from fear,
And sharing a peace God-given.

# NOT EVEN ONCE

*(A Sonnet for Victorio Charles Suarez-Hevia*
*Upon the Occasion of his First Christmas, 1996)*

Not even once have I had a vision,
Seen God's chariot ride upon the storm,
The lion's face, the eagle, ox—the man—
The winged beasts, the eyes with precision
Casting this way and that over the form
The exile took, over the grief that ran
To numbness, lack of will, self-derision;
Yet I have seen cold poles of power warm,
The bear head home, the proud bird perch, the span
Contract, worlds no longer in collision
Laugh, the man stand by, brutal pain the norm
Of her ascent—to birth the Child, the Lamb—
The woman cry, "*Magnificat*," the Child,
The Father's breath upon his cheek, exiled.


NOTE: See Ezekiel 1:1,4–6, 10–12, 15–20; Luke 1:46–55.

# A SHEPHERD'S CAROL

*(For Miguel and Mateo Suarez-Hevia—Advent, 2005)*

Why do the heavens ring
  As with choired song?
Why do the hills rejoice
  And the song prolong?
Why does a father's eye
  Hold a mother's tear
  At her baby's cry?
Why do I wonder why?

Why does the trembling earth
  Fill with wild war song?
Why do the nations rage
  And the song prolong?
Why must a father's eye
  Hold a mother's tear,
  Watch her baby die?
Why do I wonder why?

Why does my soul yet thrill
  To the heavenly song,
Still all the rage of war,
  Heaven's song prolong?
Why does a baby's cry
  Clear a mother's tear
  From a father's eye?
Why do I wonder why?

## SONNET IN REMEMBRANCE
## OF PAN AMERICAN FLIGHT 103

*(Crashed December 21, 1988)*

Flight 103 went off the radar screen,
A silent signal of swift, certain doom
For those aboard her, and for others, gloom
To overwhelm the season, calm, serene
In which she fell. The happy Christmas green,
The festive, red poinsettias in full bloom,
The fire-warmed cheer that filled the living room
All failed. Yet, from out this grief-stricken scene,
The scattered bones of innocents, the cries
Of mourning, rage draws voice, and claims its chance
To hear the Christmas requiem, fleshed Word
Divine now crashed to earth with tears, and sighs
Too deep for words, that mournful prayers might dance
Before their God, and there, by grace, be heard.

## THE BAPTIZED

They die with him for whom he died,
And live with him to die no more.

# THE PAUSE

*(Thoughts upon Recovery from Surgical Anesthesia)*

A dreamless sleep,
An eternity lost,
An unsensed silence
Shaped at the bier of memory.

## AUTOPSY

*(John 3:6a)*

The body's dead,
The brain's decayed,
The mind is dust,
The self is crushed.
"What is born of the flesh is flesh."

## ENTRÉE

*(John 3:6b)*

Now the curtain of flesh is rent
And the holiest of holies
Prowls the precincts of the soul,
Terrorizing doubt with raw belief.
"What is born of the Spirit is spirit."

# SONNET FOR A SLEEPLESS NIGHT

*(Psalm 127:2, KJV)*

I read: "He giveth his beloved sleep,"
And, sleepless, shall I wonder without rest
If I'll not join the banquet of the blest
But dine instead in Dive's dive, and weep
To see loved Lazarus and those who keep
The feast far off, my having failed some test
I took all unawares, some noble quest
I shunned perhaps; or, restless, shall I sweep
Down through that seasoned heritage of thought
My life's been spent in eating up and find
There yet untasted morsels, rare delights,
Love's promises still kept, not sold or bought,
Not up for sale, but true enough to bind
Me fast, awake, asleep through all my nights?

## THE DOGWOOD STAYS

*(A Sonnet for Good Friday)*


The dead dogwood shone in the steady sun,
In ebony and red it shone, no leaves,
No blossoms hinting life within. What grieves
The human heart: An inner life undone,
A soul's dark night grown long from having won
Its final round with reasoned hope—fine sieves
To strain from thought what vanity believes—
The soulless bark sustains. But lest we shun
With careless disregard a holy sign,
That other tree of death that shines in rays
Eternal as the sun, its ebony
Stained red with life's blood strained through veins divine,
And so lose hope entire, the dogwood stays
Encroaching dark with brightened memory.


NOTE: Legend has it that the cross of Christ was hewn of dogwood.

# GOOD FRIDAY NIGHT THOUGHTS

(To Judas—Matthew 26:20–25)

Groping is all there is in darkness,
So you grope for a way out,
For him, for yourself, for us.
I don't blame you!
The ground has shifted too much
For being unafraid.
Tomorrow God is the answer;
Tonight He is the question.

(Pilate to Jesus—Mark 15:1–5)

Here you seem so much otherwise
Than I thought you would be:
Putting darkness for light, evil for good,
And silence for sound.
Why, when I ask of you only what you
Once asked of your friends concerning yourself,
Do you keep your peace?

(For Peter—Mark 14:66–72)

He followed at a distance,
Not wanting to be found out,
Denying that he knew him,
Denying himself.
What would you have done, bard?
Sing if you must your brave songs
In the safety of here and now.
It was harder then when the cross
Was real and wood, and it bore you,
Not you it.

(It is Enough—John 19: 17–19)

He came in "silent night."
And went silent in night.

# AN EASTER HYMN

*(John 8:36)*

The budding earth in spring,
The snow bird on the wing,
The lilies bright and gay,
The frantic squirrel's play,
The happy children's songs,
Our setting right of wrongs,
The laughter in the air
That circumscribes despair,
The old men's hopeful smiles,
Young women's latest styles,
The "He is ris'n!" we shout
To quiet anxious doubt—
These do not free our life
From secret fears and strife.
No, elsewhere we must look
For hope we're not forsook
And left to face the end
Alone, without a friend,
Condemned by our own scorn,
Without one word that's born
Of love we can't explain
Or manage to obtain
Through effort of our own,
It's being free and thrown
Our way. We look to one
Who calls himself the Son,
Takes on our fear, our strife,
Frees us to share his life.

# DAYDREAM COWBOY

*(Readington Fields, New Jersey)*

The fields lay waiting for the boy's brave romp.
The goat was in her pen, the chickens cooped.
The setter, Rusty, having had his run,
Inside the house, was stretched upon his mat
Close by the kitchen door. Upon the stoop
The boy became a cowboy, saddled up,
And herding cattle over trails to towns
Where he defended honor with a gun
So fast upon the draw it drew no glint
Of sun, but chased off threat without a shot.
The bigger boys with bully fists, the girls
With bully tongues were not seen in these parts.
Day-dreamy boys around here ruled the roost
And romped with dreamy eye the waiting fields.

## SONNET ON A SOUL'S DESCENT

My soul when young would dance across the sky,
And sing among the Pleiades a song
So sweet, so bright, the stars all sang along,
A canticle of praise to God on high.
The planets with their moons joined in to cry
Their hallelujahs, a cherubic throng
To overwhelm and silence every wrong
Of earth's deep night, and quiet every lie.
But then the sisters' griefs became my own.
Through galaxies of loss my soul plunged down
To halt among sad Sheol's shadowed forms.
My canticle of praise became a groan
The heavenly hallelujahs could not drown,
And deep earth's furies shrieked through skyless storms.

# UNCLE LOUIE

*(Memorial Minute for a Life Lost in World War II)*

Uncle Louie lost his life
In Okinawa
Long before he died,
Lost it trucking prisoners
When he shot–point blank–
A lunging captive
Destined for a prison camp
Where he'd have been kept safe.

Occupied Okinawa
Sealed my uncle's fate,
Occupied his mind, his soul,
Wiped away his smile,
Trucked off every bit of him
That love could care to hold.
Gone for good the games he'd led;
Gone the quips, the tease;
Gone rides in his laundry truck,
Me pretending I could steer.

Uncle Louie died of a stroke
Thirty years ago,
A twisted smile on his lips,
Body, mind, and soul
Occupied no more.
Safely camped among the dead,
Like the prisoner he'd shot–
Point blank–Uncle Louie lies:
His life, lost and missed so long . . .
Found in this my song.

# HEADING WEST ON THE JERICHO TURNPIKE

*(January 25, 2003, 5:05 PM, for Dana Charry)*

Down the slope
> of a winter wood
>> wind-cleared thicket
>>> dead leaves scattered

The sun roiled
> at the horizon
>> a howling brilliance
>>> soon to flame out

White noise
> to the deaf ear
>> of turnpike traffic
>>> eager for Jericho.

## SONNET ON GRIEF

I think I'd rather curse my God and die
Than bear the empty silence grief imparts
To those who cannot grieve, whose grieving starts
No flow of thought, no feeling deep or high,
No fretting for what might have been, no sigh,
No discontent, no working of the arts
Of grief, no poetry of rage, no darts
Of perfect hate. So venture this: to try
The silence with a silence dreadful, still,
A still-life gesture, vacant, dumb and cold,
Indifferent, vast and deep as silent night,
More quiet, more reserved, more stark, more chill
Than death. I'd grieve grief with a silence bold,
A curse on empty night till God speaks light.

## CAPITAL IDOL

*(Matthew 16:26)*

Just as I am,
Why should I plea?
Is it not plain
God's pleased with me?
I've riches, I've celebrity.
I've won! O lamb that I am, I've won!

## CONFESSION WITHOUT APOLOGY

Of course I've spoken harsh words time to time,
And time to time I've had them said to me.
It's when the angry fever starts to climb,
You've felt it, I am sure, that boiling sea
Within that stirs up meanness in a man,
The need to take revenge, make someone pay,
That sets a man to fixing on a plan
To do in all his enemies one day.
But the blessed day for getting even
Never comes. So, you bet, harsh words, off aim,
Spit out without thought to cool the fever,
I've had my share. Life's not even steven.
Tough luck if you're the one to catch the blame,
Feel the heat, be my fever's reliever.

# AN UNAUTHORIZED LAMENT

*(Jeremiah 8:22)*

The blood of the republic drains
From every rivulet and stream
Down aging, sclerotic rivers
To an ever-rising sea,
And the wounded shores retreat
Toward a barely beating heartland.
The fathers of the nation weep;
Mothers, who labored hard to birth
A commonwealth that came to scorn
Maternal benevolence,
Can bring the body politic
No tender hope of healing.
And the oath-sworn, cheered elect,
Charged at least to do no harm,
Wills not to hear a still, small wail
From the throat of pallid empire.
The prophetic pulse weakens.
"Is there no balm in Gilead?
Is there no physician there?"
The land, sickened by its blood loss
Does not rise to ask.  Cannot care.

# THE WOUND DRESSER
*(Jeremiah 6:14)*

Bleeding hearts cascaded
Over the old stone wall,
Years of ruin shaded
By the delicate fall
Of blossomed sympathy.
No human wound dresser
Patched with healing beauty
These rock fissures.  Pressure
Upwards from seeds bursting
With glory, after rain,
Brought this deep, glad healing,
Tenderness not in vain.
It's more than passing strange
That human hate should score
Its walls of flesh, and change
To careless metaphor
The healed rock wall's beauty:
"Curse those damned bleeding hearts!"
The flowers wither, see?
A change in nature starts.
Fissured walls of flesh groan,
Revealing hearts of stone.

## MELANCHOLY

The slate sky sags
Like a tired roof,
Threatening the house.

Inside, alone, at the kitchen window
The old man struggles
To sit up, to look out.

"Sit up, sit up straight,"
He hears her say,
"Or you'll end up stooped for good."

The old man's heart,
Heavy as the sky,
Cannot obey.

# WHEN I GREW UP

*(A Sonnet Dedicated to the Memory*
*of G. Robert Jacks, d. 5 June 2002)*

When I grew up I lost the worlds of cloud
My summer daydreams conjured in the sky.
No time to waste, I up and let them die
And turned to face the world the facts allowed,
The world of purposes and plans that crowd
Our days with "have to do," for we must ply
Those trades that make the world go round, and shy
Away from dream-filled hours. Yet though I vowed
To work—and dream no more—lost worlds came back
When summer clouds rained grief into my toil.
Now all my purposes and plans were spent.
The facts gave way to sums no math could track.
My grown-up world was left to age and spoil,
And wasted daydreams saw their heavens rent.

## FOR MY MOTHER-IN-LAW, RUTH MITCHELL GOETSCHIUS, UPON THE OCCASION OF HER EIGHTY-FIFTH BIRTHDAY

*(February 12, 1987)*

To some you are my mother-in -law
By law's decree,
By the vows that bind me fast
"For better or worse," to your daughter,
Cast, without consent or desire, into my life,
Having neither rhyme nor reason
Why this should be so,
Your future, present, past
Blended with mine
By fate, time, chance
To last a marriage out.

Yet the question "Why?" I know
Never concerned you,
Nor did fate, time, chance
Once cross your mind,
Nor did rule of law count for much
In your mothering of me.
No, all was done for love,
For love that kindled love
And in me saw at last
Its offspring, son,
Born glad and free.

# SONNET IN HONOR OF A MAN OF GOD

*(For Thomas W. Gillespie)*

May I provide a Festschrift all my own
To celebrate what in you He has done
Who sought no prizes and no laurels won,
Whose seed of sure and steadfast love was sown
In weeds of hate and ignorance? Alone
He faced the way of sorrow, He, the Son
The Father kissed and sent to be undone
For sin's undoing. Now above the groan
Of wasted lives, the mortal wounds, the tears
All generations know, and through the schemes
Devised to hide the guilt of deicide,
One hears His voice. He called you in your fears
To brave humility, to speak the dreams
He spoke, in you to have his seed abide.

## A LONE, PATIENT, KEEN-EYED HAWK

A lone, patient, keen-eyed hawk
Perched upon my locust limb
Waits and watches where I sit
As if some prey, a chipmunk
Or a rabbit, might appear
From the dark grove of spruce trees
At my back. I am perplexed.
The chipmunk's home's the stone wall
Across the yard. The rabbit
Is nestled near the lilacs,
Underneath the peony
By the fern. Here I'm alone,
Waiting, watching, while the hawk
Patient on his locust limb,
Keen-eyed, still, is watching me.

## JUST DESSERT

The blackberries I used to pick
Out back among the apple trees and poison ivy
Were wild and sweet as any boy could want them.
One by one, with care,
I placed them in my wooden-handled pot.
"There," I said,
"And don't get crushed and juiced too soon,
Or by the time you reach the pie I picked you for
You'll not be worth my trouble or my mom's.
She wants you whole and dark
And so do I.
You're best that way,
Not gone to matted seed."
The berries gave no answer.
But from the way each rested still
It seemed that what I said was heard.
The berries, every one, obeyed my word:
The proof was in the pie.
And so I was content with berry picking,
Content enough not to mind the poison ivy rash
That came and itched my arms so badly
Only shortly after all the pie was gone
And I was on my way to bed.
The taste was earned with itch,
And that sufficed for justice.
To wish for more than that,
No itch at all or all untroubled sleep,
Would be to beg for grace
Which can't be gotten for the asking
Or the earning,
But which is given for human need
When what has gone to seed

*(continued on p. 48)*

Is not just blackberries in a pot or pie,
But life itself.
Days crushed and juiced to tears
From weight of years desperate for grace
Come all too soon.
Fools beg them on
With an itch for more than they deserve.
But wise folk, without a sigh,
Settle for justice and blackberry pie.

# REMEMBRANCE AND REUNION

*(In Honor of the Bound Brook, New Jersey,*
*High School Class of 1955)*

Their hallway lockers stand in silent rows
Like monuments to mark the graves of saints
Interred in ancient ruins of the mind,
Their names long gone, erased by daily storms
That cloud the common memory with grief,
And turn to dust attempts to claim the past
As comfort for the present; Yet we meet,
And not as mourners meet to grieve the dead
With hymns to praise them, fight songs for the lost;
As heirs we meet to claim each other's joy,
And trace in aging faces lines of grace
And seams of laughter, wealth enough to last
Till time itself is past, and storms are spent,
And Peace inters us with the saints in hope.

## DUST AND PRAYER

*(Genesis 2:7)*

God breathed into the dust a prayer,
And made of what he'd stirred up there
An image of himself, we're told,
A creature of the dust, ensouled.

## EVERY WORD

Every word was once a prayer
Born of hope or else despair,
Of yearning for what's not yet seen,
Of sighing for what might have been.

## AN OLD CONUNDRUM

Who says, "I can't believe
What's not been proved,"
Forgets that what's been proved
Can't be believed.

## THE FUTURE PRESENT TENSE

The future comes in winter as in spring,
With nightfall just as surely as with dawn,
A first breath catching life, a last breath drawn
In failing gasps, brief labored sighs that bring
Death down to life, a beauty made to fling
Its summer warmth upon cold hates that spawn
In falls of fear, a blight upon the lawn
Once green with hope where love could walk and sing.
There's no one ever saw the future clear
No matter what the season. No one felt
The earth's core cool, or heard the crack of ice
That meant the melting of the poles was near.
The future came as change endured, and dwelt
In us: A present tense that must suffice.

## ON "THE PERFORMED SELF
IS THE ONLY SELF THERE IS"

All there is to me is what I'm put through,
Some would say, or what I myself would do
To counter what's been done, to hold in view
A prospect of what I somehow could be
If all there was, was possibility,
A freedom to imagine, and to see
Imagination's vision once come true,
Just once, to get what I thought I was due,
And not to settle for what others knew
Was only right and good and just for me,
What I was titled to by birth, or fee
Paid to square my debt to society.
But then, a self's breath, old, a word to toll
Through ages: Adam made a living soul!

# I NEVER THOUGHT MYSELF

*(After reading scholarly articles on "Performance Studies")*

I never thought myself a learned man,
Nor unlearned, never wise nor unwise,
Never easily comprehending all
Nor uneasily missing everything,
Never certain that I was always right,
Nor uncertain that I was often wrong,
Never altogether sure nor unsure;
But now am I absolutely baffled,
More, daunted, to read in learned journals
The play of "Who am I?" and "What is it?"
As mental hide and seek, where no one hides,
And no one seeks, and no one ever finds,
And no one minds that in this darkened glass
Of text, I think not, and therefore am not.

## A LESSON LEARNED
## IN MRS. FISHER'S KINDERGARTEN

In kindergarten I liked best the cars
I got to pedal round the room alone.
My favorite car was red and white, with chrome;
And Mrs. Fisher said I drove it well,
For I was careful not to hit the cars
My classmates drove, though they, it seems, were fond
Of hitting me. They'd chase me down, and slam
Into my rear as if to say: "Get out,
Out of my way, out of my school, my town!"
And I'd have gotten out had I the chance.
But I was only four, and in *my* town
The kindergarten age was set at five.
So stuck in angry traffic I learned young
To pedal hard and steer as best I could.

## CANCER VIGIL

*(A Sonnet in Memory of John Wesley Goetschius, Who Died of Adenocarcinoma and Mesothelioma; Composed in the Hours Before his Death, January 2, 2001)*

*For in hope we were saved. Now hope that is seen is not hope. For who hopes for what is seen? But if we hope for what we do not see, we wait for it with patience (Romans 8:24–25, NRSV).*

There is no room for hosts of angels now
To wage their holy war on Satan's horde,
For now the cosmic course of death is toward
The finite body which does not allow
Infinity in burning form a proud,
Seraphic flight against the dreaded lord.
Here darkened, microscopic paths afford
Frail molecules of care the chance to plough
Through fevered cells a chastened hope of life
Beyond the sting of death, and nothing more.
All grander measures are of no avail.
Heroic interventions prolong strife.
For cancers of this type there's no known cure.
Death wins, yet in the winning still shall fail.

# THE PLUMBER: A REMEMBRANCE

Large hands and larger heart,
Strong back and stronger will,
A laborer, for love of life,
And love of them who on this earth still
Wonder: did he choose the better part?

He would not say such words himself,
But thought them, I suppose,
For don't we all?
Too busy joining pipe to pipe
And year to year for pay.

But more than once he did say—
I know, I heard him—
"Prestige? A man can't eat prestige.
Give me a job that pays, for work's for living."
And live he did, and loved to live each day.

He lived the day he died,
Not grumbling: "Well, I'm near the end,"
Then seeking out some hand to hold or wring.
This man was a laborer, so he went working.
No one was at his side. That was his way.

## FOR AUNT BILL

*(A Salutation and Valediction)*

Aunt Bill hid under the dining room table
Whenever strangers came to the front door
And no one else was home to ask, "Who's there?"
Hunkered secure beneath her sturdy oak,
Floor-draped with a cloth of antique linen,
She listened till the nameless ringing stopped.
She held her breath. Then, convinced by stillness
That all was well and that the dining room
Once more could be trusted with her secret,
She breathed again, crept from her oaken refuge,
And laid claim to a quiet victory.
She smiled. Whose business was it anyway
That she preferred the known to the unknown,
How it was to the way that it could be?

# THE WORD GOD SENT

*(John 1:1, 14 RSV)*

"In the beginning was the Word."
But shuffling, thumb-noise knowledge,
Heedless truth,
Unpersoned language,
Neat stained upon white sheets,
Indifferent leaves,
Symbols writ in man's own image,
Silent, self-contained and self-concerned,
Thrown back upon themselves in endless loops,
Cut off the world of sense and sight and mind
From mystery and myth.
Imagination stalled.
ABC encoded all.
Two plus two became a faith, and man a fact.
So shrunk from what he could not see or hear,
Impaled upon himself,
He died to God.

"And the Word became flesh."
Dwelt among cold calculations,
Battling minds that figured all there was and all there was to be,
Declaring thought the servant, not the master of the race,
Crossing possible to probable
With upstart beam of "What if?" and "Could be."
Crucified by men reduced, predictable, aghast,
Crying out, forgiving, slumped in death,
There hung the Word uncomfortably stretched in human form,
And poet sense declared, "Behold the man."

*(continued on p. 61)*

"And we have beheld his glory,"
Glory as of God's-own-Son-man,
Unpresuming, unassuming,
And in stature, indiscernible by rod,
Gracing sanctuary song and sawmill,
Leper, legion, leader, lacky,
Marriage feast, and family strife
With all of hope belief in love can bring.
Dissatisfied, he leaves us,
Only Spirit marks to guide us
To expanse of knowing awe and derring-do.

# THE ALPHA AND THE OMEGA

*(Revelation 21:1–6a)*

Who could have imagined
That darkness was as light,
That evening's breath was bright
With music of the dawn,
Was blest with silence drawn
Through Spirit lips to sing:
"I am the Beginning
And the End, who fashioned
Day and night, the laughter
Of sun-split clouds after
Rain, all the forms of mirth
That dance throughout the earth,
Not least, eternity,
With human beings free
From their grief and sorrow,
Their hate and their narrow
Loyalties, their faces
Radiant with traces
Of God's own glad image,
Glory's smiling visage?"
Who could have imagined,
Creation's end in view,
All souls, all things, made new?

# RECTIFICATION

The wind-wrecked aspen's tattling tongues are still,
And thorny locust limbs are strewn about
To prick the careless hand that grips them bare.
Our cleaning up of this year's autumn storms
Will not be fun. It seems we're over-matched
By nature's ruin of what nature's bred
And planted, watered, warmed, and caused to grow.
The seasons change; but one thing stays the same,
The work of setting right what's gone all wrong
In nature: this unreckonable waste.
It's more than we can tackle on our own,
Try as we may. The rectifying deed
Is out of our control. It takes a strength
No human strength's attained or ever will.

## AS A MOTHER COMFORTS

*(Isaiah 66:13)*

Lord most dear,
Are you near,
Can you hear
Me crying?

I'm your child,
Gloom-beguiled;
Dreams gone wild,
I'm dying.

Mother-love,
Promised dove,
From above
Still crying:

"Comfort!" O
Toll, toll, toll,
In my soul
Death's dying!

# A SEASONED GRATITUDE

Late autumn dusk
Along the abandoned canal
Was Renoir through isinglass.
My eyes, all crystalline opacity,
Blurred the fine-edged
Impressionist glory of nature.
I will not say diminished it,
For ocular cataracts,
Though unwelcome,
Are the lens of old age,
And one is glad
To live long enough
To grow them. I see,
Not clearly, but sufficiently well
To relish the delicate blends
Of obscured colors
That once dazzled.
I will come here often,
Happy that diminished powers of sight
Are enhanced by memory.
And I will be grateful
For this abandoned canal,
For autumn dusk, for Renoir,
And for isinglass.

## THE STUDENT TO HIS BELOVED

*(A Villanelle Composed with Fond Remembrance
of Grade School Music Teacher, Edna Tittler)*


I strive to learn against a mind too slow.
From childhood on I fell behind in fear,
My life *vivace*, but my thoughts *largo*.

It's true one learns by failing, still I know
That failing without learning brings a tear.
I strive to learn against a mind too slow.

My music teacher once gave hope and cheer,
But she's long dead, and all my years speed on,
My life *vivace*, but my thoughts *largo*.

Now you, beloved, cheer my thoughts, although
My hope of catching up seems all but gone.
I strive to learn against a mind too slow.

Yet this one thing to you and me seems clear:
The time we have together is not done,
The tempo set *vivace* or *largo*.

Together we will try somehow to know
Much more than can be known of love, though dear,
I strive to learn against a mind too slow,
My life *vivace*, but my thoughts *largo*.

## SALVATION

As with a powerful but unseen blow,
Midwinter's sun strikes every tree in sight.
Ice-sheathed limbs, bravely *engarde*, glistening, bright,
Wildly flail. Armor falls into the snow—
Shoulder pieces, elbow plates, gauntlets glow
Then disappear. Bare tree bark, dark as night,
Stands exposed to day. All is brought to light:
The wounds, the tears that let the sweet sap flow.
Yet warrior light, fierce as unseen grace,
Saves what it strips that's armored unto death
With slash after slash, silent, certain, keen.
Swift, sure, assault upon assault with pace,
The beauty of it makes us catch our breath,
And wish for light ourselves to strip us clean.

# THE PRAISE AND THE GLORY

I doubt we'll ever forget
The meadow we passed just yesterday
Tatted with webs dew drenched
And glistening in the sun.
You and I remarked
We'd never seen the like before.
It seemed to us that Charlotte
Must have called a convention of her peers
To fashion, not for us, of course,
But for her and for themselves,
This scene, this acreage of silent praise.
And it came to me,
To you as well, I know,
Though you never spoke of it,
But only smiled your assent:
Who would have thought
That such delicate and unintended art
Should bear such a weight of glory?

## Stranger Dust

"What about writing an afterword for my book of poems—something about what gets made of a poem once others get a hold of it?" my dad suggested. "*Not* a literary critique," he quickly added—he knows my limitations—"more like a response to the notion that once a poem is out there, it is left to the reader, the speaker, the hearer to make what she will of it." I loved the idea for two reasons. First, I would have six weeks of summer off as an elementary-school teacher, so in theory I would have enough time to write it. Second, I simply looked forward to immersing myself in my dad's poetry. I was familiar enough with his work to know that immersing myself in it would be like wrapping myself in the folds of his black preacher's robe as a little girl. Back then I would peek out at the parishioners shaking his hand or, more commonly, hide behind his legs in the robe's silky coolness, soothed and protected. I knew I could use some soothing and protection now, and I knew good poetry and good writing, his poetry and his writing, offered me that.

So perhaps that is what I make out of his poetry, or what it becomes for me, a shelter from "fierce heat and cold," a vista point from which to view a valley with its fertile soil " . . . washed down from heights long dead, but for the stir of wind . . . ." But that's not all. It's not that the poet is gone when I read his words and I'm left alone to make something of them. No. The poet is there in the moment of the reading, a real presence. And the reader is there, a more tangible presence, acting on the poet's work. And though I am indeed making something of the poems, even more they are making something of me. In the moments shared between the reader and the poem—and thus the poet—something inexplicably new is stirred to life, the reader herself perhaps.

Anne Lamott writes, "My gratitude for good writing is unbounded. I'm grateful for it the way I'm grateful for the ocean." That is how I feel about this book of poetry.

Rebecca J. Bartow
San Ramon, CA
August 10, 2007